Paul Wilson Schaughency

KITTY CRIDER

ISBN 979-8-89043-491-3 (paperback)
ISBN 979-8-89043-492-0 (digital)

Christian Faith Publishing
832 Park Avenue
Meadville, PA 16335
www.christianfaithpublishing.com

Printed in the United States of America

I would like to tell you some of the lucky things that have happened to me in my lifetime. First of all, I was born September 14, 1921, three days before my mother's forty-first birthday. I understand that back in the 1920s, not many women were having babies past the age of forty. I'm lucky to *be* here!

Beaver, Pennsylvania

THE FIRST THING I remember happened just before my third birthday.

Paul Schaughency, circa 1923

Mother's brother, my uncle Lester, who'd hit it pretty big in oil, sent Mother train tickets for the two of us to go out to Denver, Colorado, for a visit. I remember one incident on the trip. We were in a Pullman (sleeping) car. Mother and I shared a berth at night. I was in bed alone and crying. The porter, hearing my crying, stuck his head through the curtain and said, "Don't cry, little boy. Don't cry. Your mama's just down in the bathroom at the end of the car.

She'll be right back." That's all I remember about the train trip. She returned almost immediately, and all was well.

After we got to Denver, I remember looking out their kitchen window and seeing some big mountains. I asked, "Is that Pike's Peak?"

I was told, "No, Pike's Peak is further south, and you can't see it from here." Those are two things I remember from that trip. I think I'm lucky to remember that bit from that young age.

One day in February 1932, when I was in fifth grade, the two elementary schools (k–6) were to meet at the high school auditorium for a program. I was selected over the other sixth graders to give the introductory speech. I remember the first line, "This year of 1932 marks the bicentennial of the birth of George Washington." The program was about Washington.

The next lucky break happened when I was in the Boy Scouts. In 1935, they were having the National Jamboree. It was to be in Washington, D.C., and I *really* wanted to go. The fee was $25 for the week. This was during the Depression, and I prayed that somehow my family could get the fee together. I talked to my mother with a proposition. I had $5; both my brothers were working. If they each gave me $5, the family only needed to come up with $10. I didn't get much reaction from Mother. The deadline passed, and I still didn't have the $25. I prayed some more. I almost lost my religion. Then President Roosevelt canceled the Jamboree because of a polio epidemic in Washington, D.C. So instead of being disappointed, I was lucky I didn't go. (The polio vaccine hadn't been discovered yet.)

The next interesting happening came when I was in high school. I had to go to see the school superintendent whose office was in the high school. He had called me in to talk about the gift that our class was going to give the school upon graduation. I was president of the junior class and had just been elected to be president of the senior class. The then-senior class had committed to gifting the school $300. He wanted us to match it. We did this by filling the auditorium for our senior class play! If we gifted $300 plus the $300 from the previous class, the school board would match it. This would be used for a new Hammond organ. Just as I was leaving, he said,

"Paul, I think you would do well in personnel work." At the time, I didn't know what he was talking about.

Senior picture from 1939 Beaver High School Yearbook

University of Pittsburgh

I RECEIVED AN honors scholarship to the University of Pittsburgh. The registrar came to interview me. They were looking for not only grades (top 10 percent of the class) but also activities which I had quite a few. At freshman registration at Pitt, I was assisted by my hometown friend, Bill Donaldson, who was then a sophomore. At the end of the line, I was asked, "Gym or ROTC?"

I asked Bill, "What did you take?"

He said, "Well, if you take gym you have to go up to Trees Gym, on the top of the hill on the far side of Pitt Stadium. Then if your next class is down at the Cathedral of Learning, you have to hurry to get down there. You might as well not have taken a shower. It's just a hassle. I took ROTC."

I said, "Bill, what's that?"

He replied, "Reserve Office Training Corps. In case of a war, you go as a second lieutenant, instead of a buck private." I was thinking about the long trek up the hill, and I took ROTC. On the first of September, Hitler crossed the Molotov-Von Ribbentrop line violating the treaty dividing Poland between Russian and German areas of influence. Our country was divided as to helping the Europeans against Hitler. The draft act of 1940 had been passed by only one vote. A group called American Firsters was against going over to help Europe again. I wasn't concerned about the war. Deciding on ROTC was a really lucky break, let me tell you.

I was a junior, so I was going into advanced ROTC, but first I had to pass a physical. I took it. The next day, Lt. Husband of the ROTC faculty called me at the fraternity house where I had just finished serving lunch. He told me that I didn't pass the physical and that he had made arrangements for me to take it again. My heartbeat was too fast. I asked what do I need to do? He replied that I needed to get a good night's sleep. I went and everything was fine. That was September 1941. I was lucky to be admitted into advanced ROTC.

Then on December 7, 1941, the Japanese bombed Pearl Harbor. We were at war. The first class after that, the colonel came and, in his southern accent, said, "Now, boys, there will be enough heroes running off to join the Air Corps. Your Uncle Sam wants you to stay and get your education. Instead of going to the usual six-week summer camp, you'll go to officer candidate school and then receive your commission."

We all talked among ourselves (tongue in cheek) if Uncle Sam wants us to stay and get our education, I guess we'd better do it.

Because I was in advanced ROTC, when the war came, my decision, my freshman year of not going up that hill, really paid off. I am a lucky guy.

The army asked us to go to summer school. Some of us couldn't go because we needed to work for college expenses. They allowed it, which was lucky for me.

I was in the school of business administration. In our junior and senior years, the required courses were few so that you could take the courses in your area of concentration.

By this time, I should have selected an area of concentration, but I hadn't. I knew where I was going—the army with a guarantee of going to OCS. I planned to graduate with a general business administration degree.

At the end of our senior year, we received orders to go to New Cumberland, Pennsylvania, Reception Center for processing into the active army. Then the orders said we were assigned to Fort Eustis, Virginia, for basic training and later assigned to OCS. Talk about a bunch of grumbling guys, "When is this *later*?" "They promised we were going to OCS," "What is this basic training at Fort Eustis?"

Well, we started basic training at Fort Eustis. We were part of the first half-track antiaircraft battalion. The antiaircraft guns were mounted on the back of the half-track, something new for our army. At the end of the first month, our class was taken out of basic training and sent to Seacoast Artillery OCS at Fort Monroe, Virginia. Part of our class at Fort Monroe was from the Citadel. Our guys said, "*Wow*! The Citadel! That's the west point of the south, and they are getting the same treatment as we are." All the complaints from the ex-Pitt soldiers stopped.

We finished our OCS, received our second lieutenant commission, and graduated on November 19, 1943.

In the Army

Lt. Paul W. Schaughency

I GOT MY first choice of Fort Hancock, New Jersey. (It was the nearest to Pittsburgh.) However, they didn't tell you what unit you were assigned to, just the post. I joined a Florida National Guard outfit. They had been alerted for overseas. We didn't know if we were going to Europe or to the Pacific. Our Florida National Guard unit was to be sent to Alaska.

I had asked Katie to come down for Christmas. She called me saying neither of her sisters could be home for Christmas, and she couldn't leave her parents alone for the holiday. She added that she could come for New Year's. New Year's Eve was on Friday that year. We decided on Thursday to get married. I could get a three-day pass and could have the wedding on the following Tuesday. I said to Katie, "I guess I'm supposed to talk to your father about this." So I called him. I said, "Katie and I are talking about getting married. I guess I need your blessing."

He asked, "When? Of course, it's okay, but when?" I put her on the phone to talk to her father. She said she'd like to have it at the East Liberty Presbyterian Church (where they were members), in the chapel. I had seen the chapel. It's as nice as some small churches.

I had two brothers and no sisters, so didn't know about the wedding stuff.

I hear her pondering about some sorority sisters, remembering aloud that two of them were in the same wedding. They have dresses that are alike, and Weezie can be my maid of honor because she was at another wedding, so she'll have a dress. I said to her, "Oh, I see that it is important about being dressed alike, so I guess I'd better see about the best man and the two ushers." She agreed. I said, "I know Bill Donaldson and Paul DeMerit are in med school and are both in the navy, so they'll have uniforms alike. I know my roommate, Dal Heim, has a tux because he had one at the senior dance." I called Pitt med school for Bill Donaldson. I was told Dr. Donaldson had been called to active duty and was now in Long Beach, California. I thought, *I guess that won't work.* I got Paul DeMerit and a fellow who had been in Pitt Players with me, who was also in med school and the navy. So I asked him.

(The one problem that I hadn't anticipated and didn't learn about until our fiftieth reunion party. My roommate's uncle owned the tux that he'd borrowed. The uncle had been called to the service, so his tux wasn't available. He told me he had a dickens of a time getting one because of the shortages during the war. But he got one.)

I called Gertrude, my sister-in-law, my brother Ed's wife. I said, "We're planning to get married Tuesday. We'd like to have Diana as the flower girl." She was two and a half, pushing three. (Our side of the family knew what a pistol she was. She would come into the house, get on the couch, walk across the top of it, and then sit down.)

Gertrude said, "You mean *our* Diana?"

I said, "Yes, she'll be fine." And she was!

On Friday, a sergeant came up to me and said, "Lieutenant, they don't want this outfit overseas. They were alerted out at Fort Crockett, Texas, and didn't go. They went to Fort Moultrie in South Carolina, were alerted again, and didn't go. Instead, they came up here. They don't want this outfit overseas. Don't worry about it." Sergeants always know what was going on, so I wasn't really concerned about it.

Another lucky break I had was when our unit doctor came to me after the clinic closed and said, "You two kids are getting married. You know you have to have a blood test. Come down to the clinic, and I'll open up, and we'll get your blood tests." I had the blood test form that he signed.

Major Shindel, who lived across the hall from me in the officer's quarters, said, "You two get the last ferry (heading to New York City) at ten thirty. I'll sign you out after midnight." He signed me out (thus that day counted as a day of work on the front end of the three-day pass). We got a train out of NYC that night and arrived in Pittsburgh the next morning.

Now it was Monday morning, and we had to get the marriage license. We got there as soon as the place opened. The clerk at the marriage license bureau asked for the blood test form. He said, "This is on a New Jersey form," and Katie *exploded*!

I had never seen her temper before nor since, quite that bad. But she was going to rip him. She said, "Don't you know there's a war on?" I was standing there in my uniform. "Don't you know there's a war going on?"

I said, "Katie, wait a minute! Hold it! I think he's trying to tell us something." And he was.

He said, "There's an army unit at Pitt. If you take this New Jersey form to the army doctor there, ask him to transfer the information onto a Pennsylvania form. Since an army doctor signed the New Jersey form, we're in business." I did. I showed him the form, and I explained the situation. He said, "Give me that form." He filled out a PA form. We went back to the marriage license bureau with the right form and got our license.

I learned from Katie that I was supposed to get some flowers for the females of the wedding party, so I called my friend, Herb Woods, a florist in Rochester, Pennsylvania, near Beaver. I worked for him on school holidays and other days during busy times and helped with making deliveries. He said he could get the flowers for the ladies and then went on to say, "You know there are shortages, and a lot of florists don't have the *crash* for the bride to walk down the aisle on. Do you know if the florist your future father-in-law uses has a bridal aisle runner? I'll just throw a roll in my truck when I bring the bouquets."

Sure enough, we needed it. Herb had brought it along. I said, "Herb, I think that is the epitome of extravagance. That white sheet rolled down the aisle just for the bride to put her little feet on." Herb said that we had to have that, and thanks to him, we did.

Gertrude had a tough time finding a dress for Diana. She found a confirmation dress for her, and she looked just perfect.

I was telling Gertrude that Katie's wedding dress was supposed to come from her sister in New Orleans. It was supposed to be shipped air express but hadn't arrived yet. Gertrude said, "Well, maybe my dress will fit Katie. I'll bring it." When Katie put it on, it fit like a glove. Was that a lucky break!

On Tuesday, January 4, we had our wedding, and everything went sooo smoothly. The people that were supposed to be there were there, and we had a really nice dinner afterward. A very nice wedding all arranged on a three-day pass!

January 4, 1944

We got our train back to the fort and got to the post the next day. If you get there before midnight, that day counts as a day of duty, so really a three-day pass is almost five days. And we used up every bit of it.

We got back to Fort Hancock and found out we *were* shipping out. On the seventh day, Katie was on a train back to Pittsburgh, and I was on a train to Fort Lawton, Washington. The regiment went in four trains. One of the trains went through Pittsburgh. Major Shindel went through Pittsburgh. He got off the train and bought a newspaper. On the society page, it read, "The Schaughencys Reside at Hancock." He said, "Look at this. Like hell, they reside in Hancock. He's on a train to Seattle, and she's on a train back to Pittsburgh. Ho, ho, ho."

We got to Seattle and learned that Seattle was a POE (port of embarkation). We were set up for a three-day stay for units going overseas. Day one was arrival day. On day two, the records were checked (shots, supplies, personnel, and supply records) to make sure everything was ready to go. Day three was the departure day.

The regiment's main body left for Kodiak, the large island just under mainland Alaska.

Two small battalion headquarters units were left behind. I was assigned to one of them. After several more days at Fort Lawton, these two units boarded a ship that took us to the Aleutian Islands. Our unit went to Adak, and the other unit went to Amchitka, further out the chain of islands.

You know, that was pretty good—a Florida National Guard outfit being sent to Alaska. That figures!

(For an explanation of the Aleutian Islands, see "Addendum.")

It was late January 1944 when we arrived in Adak. It was snowing and very windy. One of the Key West boys, as we went down the gangplank with snow blowing in our faces said (with a bit of a Spanish accent), "Ah, just like Miami Beach!" He got a little *dig* back at the original Florida *crackers* in our unit. I thought it was clever.

I don't think I'll ever forget my first night on Adak. Being the junior officer, I was quickly assigned that night to be the duty officer. I said, "Now, what's that, and where do I go?" I was told to go down to the communications hut where there was a room with a bed for the duty officer. The sergeant would wake me up if something was needed. I was awakened. Remember, this was my first night there. The sergeant told me that he had gotten a message from the radar station. They had an unidentified object off Cape Adagdak, heading toward Cape Gigigak.

I said, "Yeah, where's that?" He got out the map and showed me. I had no more idea where Cape Adagdak was than where Timbuktu was. No, I had a little better idea from the battalion adjutant, my friend Warrant Officer Degan, telling me where Timbuktu was. But I learned Cape Adagdak was on our island, and the other cape was on Kanaga Island. I asked the sergeant what we should do, and he said, "Nothing. This happens frequently. It could be a flock of geese or something like that." But man, waking up and getting hit with two very strange-sounding places, unusual for a first night.

For about a year, during which I had several assignments to other batteries, I had various battery officer duties. This included battery B on the other side of the island at Shagak Bay, where I was the executive officer. One day, I got a phone call that the colonel wanted to see me.

When I got there, I was told that with the new point system going for the rotation of troops back to the states, work would increase. The colonel wanted me to be our personnel officer. (Degan was the adjutant, and the personnel officer was the assistant adjutant.) They initially did not fill this position because Degan had come up from being a personnel sergeant, and he felt that we didn't need it.

"We're small, and we can get along without it." But now with the point system, there were a lot of personnel work and other details. They needed a personnel officer.

Well, I didn't take that jumping up and down with joy. Firing battery guys called those *desk jockeys*, not a complimentary term. But now I was one of them.

When I started, I had a really good sergeant major. It started out with, "Is this right sergeant, and where do I sign?" I paid attention to what was going on, and I learned a lot, and I began to like it. The post headquarters must have noticed what I was doing because I was called to be the post personnel officer at the post headquarters. This position called for a captain, so I got a promotion too. That was a really lucky break for me, and I discovered my personnel career in the army!

After V-E Day, units were redeployed back to the US for the war against Japan. That resulted in more personnel work.

After the bomb was dropped, and the war was over, I figured I had about nine months before I could get out of the army. I was told that I could bring back my dependent if I had a year left. So I signed up for another year and asked Katie if she wanted to come over. She said, "Yes!" That was another lucky break—Katie with me, a great career, and the GI bill!

I kept saying "Katie" and that was what she was until she came up to the Aleutians with me.

Addendum

The Aleutian Islands

THE ALEUTIAN ISLANDS extend over one thousand miles west of the Alaska mainland. Most from the troops who were stationed on the Aleutians were closer to Japan than the lower forty-eight states. Attu is the island at the end of the chain, and Kiska is the next large one back. Those two islands were the only American soil that the Japanese held during World War II. In May 1943, in the Battle of Attu, we got our islands, Attu and Kiska, back.

Adak, where I was stationed, is about the middle of the chain. For the army, it was an army post, air base, and supply base depot (under construction). There was an Alaskan advanced command post in preparation for a secondary attack on Northern Japan. There were infantry field artillery and coast artillery units. Also present were the usual support units: quartermaster, engineer, ordinance, and a port supported by a transportation corps port battalion.

The navy had a base there and also a fair-size repair base. In the process was the construction of ten large warehouses. The inside was the size of four basketball courts. These warehouses were also in preparation for attacking Japan.

Amchitka is a small island just east of Kiska and was their air base. It was a better place on which to build the airfield. It was the same for Attu. They built the airfield for Attu on Shemya. It was close enough that it could be seen from Attu. Shemya was the base the air corps used for bombing raids on northern Japan during World War II.

PART 2

Home Visit after the War

THE WAR WAS over, my wife was going to join me for a year, and I had found a career path I really enjoyed. All that, of course, made me very happy!

I was ready to get home, get Katie, and get back to Adak so we could begin our life together. I wanted my travel orders either by air or sea; it didn't matter which. I called my friend, the personnel officer over at navy, to see if I could get a ride on the navy four-engine plane, and I did. If you do favors for somebody, sometimes they're returned to you.

I got the plane to Seattle and met another navy guy who was seated beside me. When we got to Seattle, there was a train strike, and very few planes were going East. They suggested to him (since we were on a navy base) we should go down to the Oakland Base. So we did. He told on the way down, "Have you ever been to Fisherman's Wharf?"

I answered, "No."

He explained that they were famous for really good seafood in San Francisco. I had never before been to a seafood place where you couldn't get a steak or a hamburger. We got to Fisherman's Wharf, and there was nothing a landlubber would like on the menu. I was his guest, so I had to try something. I asked the waiter what's the least fishy fish they had. I think it was flounder. It was absolutely not fishy. Obviously, when you are at a place like that, the fish was very fresh, and it really tasted quite good. I was very pleasantly surprised. I ate fish after that. I learned that some fish are pretty doggone tasty and not fishy. This was one big thing I learned on that trip.

We checked on flights going East, and I did get one to Indianapolis. That was where I needed to go to get the orders for my leave since I only had travel orders to get to Camp Atterbury in Edinburgh, Indiana.

Katie met me there where we stayed overnight and flew to Pittsburgh the next day. When we got to Pittsburgh, it was *socked in*. The plane circled a couple of times and headed off to Cleveland. Her family was down below us; my family was down below us; the soldier boy was returning from the army for a visit, and no one got to see anyone.

We flew to Cleveland and took a train back to Pittsburgh overnight. The next morning, Katie's dad picked us up at the train station, and we went to her parents' house. We saw my family later.

My oldest brother, Chuck, had some business in New York. Katie and I went there with Chuck and his wife, Alice. While he did business, we went sightseeing. The four of us saw two new Broadway shows: *Oklahoma* and *Carousel*. Both were great! Chuck said he liked the one about the "surrey" a little better than the other one. He liked the song "Surrey with the Fringe on Top."

We had good entertainment during the several days we were in New York. One night we went to a nightclub. We had a good seat, one table away from the stage. The star was imitating Frank Sinatra. Over my left shoulder at the next table was Frank Sinatra! He was there watching the guy doing an imitation of him. I thought that was pretty *neat*.

We had a good time in New York, came back, and did a lot of visiting. My nephew, only son of Chuck and Alice, asked if I had heard on the local radio station about driving a car to California. California buyers were in the East (1946) buying cars and needed drivers to take the cars out there. (Cars were more expensive in the West.) To drive the cars West, you had to have a permanent California address. They didn't want recently discharged veterans just looking for a place to roam. They were looking for guys who needed to get to California. Of course, we fit that. Katie had a sister out there, so we had an address. That really worked well. We took my brother Chuck to Columbus where he had business. We spent the night there and then said goodbye to him.

We headed west, arrived in Seattle, and went to the terminal in our port. We learned our ship, the Liberty ship SS *George Washington*

Carver, was a merchant ship that had been converted to a hospital ship. Troop ships were busy bringing the boys home and taking supplies and replacements back. Returning to Adak on that particular ship was a nice situation. There were two other couples on the ship besides Katie and me. Both men had been on Adak also and were headed back. Major Hudgins was a supply guy. He and his wife, Grace, were both from Virginia. Grace had a thick southern drawl. She said to Katie, "Honey, you don't seem like a Katie to me. Would you mind if I called you *Caaathy?*" Of course, Katie was thrilled, and from that point on, she was Cathy.

Colonel Ware, who was the post engineer (commander of the engineer battalion), and his wife, Peg, were the other couple. Also, there was a large group (about the size of an army engineering company) of civilian craft men who worked for the post engineers.

1946 aboard the "George Washington Carver" with Colonel and Mrs. Ware and Major and Mrs. Hudgins. Paul Schaughency, left back row standing; Cathy Schaughency in the middle chair.

The day we got back to Adak, I went over to post headquarters to check in. My boss, whom I had met shortly before leaving, had suggested bringing my wife. This was because the old advanced

Alaskan Command building was opening up as dependent housing. He said, "Schaughency, what are you doing here?" I didn't understand what he meant since my orders were for forty-five days' leave. And I was getting back on the day I was supposed to get back. He explained that he'd received a telex from Seattle asking permission to talk to me about a job down there.

We said, "Okay." Nobody from Seattle had contacted me, and he was glad to have me back! Man, oh, man, was that a lucky break! On Adak, with nothing but the PX, navy ship service, and two commissaries, we didn't spend much. Thus, the money we saved became the down payment on our first house. If we had been stationed in Seattle with the wartime population and shipbuilding industry there, the prices would have taken both of our salaries to live on. We wouldn't have been able to save. On Adak, Cathy was able to work as a civilian personnel, so it worked out well for us there.

That first day, my boss also told me there would be a court-martial, and I was asked to be the defense counsel. *Wow!*

The First Year Together
in a Quonset Hut

IT WAS PRETTY nice knowing the post engineer. His wife and Cathy really hit it off. She was a former home economics teacher, and here was Cathy just brand new, learning how to be a wife, cooking, and so forth. That turned out to be a really nice arrangement. We lived in a Quonset hut, especially designed and equipped for dependent living. They lived in a home that looked more like a house.

"The Quonset hut was equipped with only a shower, sink, toilet, oil space heater, electric stove, sink and refrigerator. I built us a bed; we got living room furniture from a navy club that was no longer in use. I built us a bar, paneled the walls from wood I salvaged from somewhere, and fixed indirect lighting for the living room so that the ceiling no longer looked like a hut. I got some wood-looking tile floor for the living room (actually something to cover the existing plywood floor)" Paul Schaughency.

Adak Stories

The Cup of Sugar

THE REALLY BAD Aleutian storms were called *williwaws* by the natives. We adopted their word. The Japanese Current, which is warm, comes north in the Pacific, goes east across underneath the Aleutian Islands and south along our West Coast, and warms it up. The Bering Current comes down from the Arctic Ocean through the Bering Sea. It's a bit chilly. They meet just about Adak, and all along the Aleutians produce very high wind speeds. The wind gauge at the air base goes up to 115 miles per hour, and these winds go beyond that!

Back to Cathy, she told me she was going down to see Peg Ware because she needed a cup of sugar. I told her it was starting to blow, and the sugar could wait until tomorrow. She said she was going, and she went. The wind was blowing pretty doggone well—we were getting ready to have a williwaw. I heard this knock so I went to the door, looked out the storm entrance, and saw no one. I looked down at my feet, and there was Cathy on her hands and knees. She'd gotten out beyond the shelter of the storm entrance, and the wind had knocked her off the boardwalk and down onto the ground. She crawled back on her hands and knees to knock on the bottom of the storm entrance door. She said, "I think I'd better listen to you!"

Williwaw vs. Landing Mat
They say in the Aleutians that "the wind blows 100 miles an hour in all directions." These winds come down from the mountains which surround Aleutian airfields, are in effect gigantic downdrafts, locally called williwaws. The highest officially recorded velocity is 135 mph—this wind blew away two weather stations. This shows what happened to a steel landing mat that wasn't spiked at the end. The wind, simultaneously blasting down at an angle and running along the ground, built up a "nozzle" velocity at the edge of the mat strong enough to roll back about 50 feet of an 11th Air Force strip.

Adak Shopping

CATHY CAME HOME one day with the news that Peg would really like to have a bathtub. She did not like the shower. I told Cathy I was sure Peg's husband could find a couple of plumbers, and I happened to know where there was a bathtub. At the far end of the peninsula where our battalion headquarters had been was a bathtub. Major Shindell had a bathtub in his quarters that he had gotten from the navy. I told Colonel Ware about the tub. His men went out, got it, and installed it, and Peg was really happy.

Cathy and my mother wrote quite a bit. In one letter, Cathy told her that Peg had looked at our floor and said she'd ask Robert (Colonel Ware) if we could get some flooring. My mother wrote back and said, "Oh, you poor dears. I thought you would be roughing it, being up in the Aleutians, but I didn't have any idea you didn't have a floor in your hut!"

Civilian Life after Adak through the End of the '40s

CATHY AND I finished up our tour on Adak and came back to Pittsburgh. The GI bill was being offered. I figured that I had been an army personnel, and I wanted to learn the civilian side of this field. So I went back to school and got a master's. At Pitt, they called it industry performance, and I took all the personnel courses I could. Cathy worked at Pitt in the treasurer's office, and we commuted together.

After graduation, while looking for a job, my father-in-law asked me for a brief résumé, just a few lines. I gave it to him, which he took to work. He was the office manager at a brokerage firm and of course, knew the president. He took it to the president of the firm who called the president of Pittsburgh Plate Glass (later PPG Industries), who was building up their industrial relations department. I was told to call the director of industrial relations. I called, made the appointment, and talked to Sam Burke, the corporate director of industrial relations. He turned me over to a person on his staff for an interview. He sent me out to a consultant for a battery of tests, and I was interviewed there. When I came back to PPG, they made me a job offer in their training program. It was to be for one year then out to one of the plants.

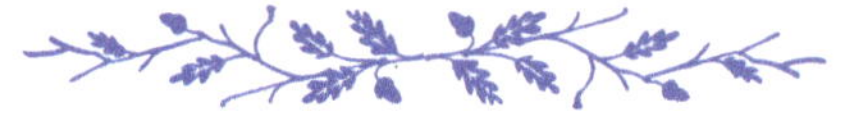

The '50s

MY PLANT ASSIGNMENT was the Pittsburgh Plate Glass plant in Mt. Vernon, Ohio. The general office thought the plant needed a little help out there. I started as training director, running supervisory training programs. I was also the secretary for the *third-step* union-management meeting with the union committee, plant manager, and department superintendent, and, of course, a secretary to take and write minutes. That experience got me into labor relations. At Mount Vernon, I figured one significant contribution I made was getting a new maintenance agreement with the union. A lot of irritating labor problems were solved. I also introduced public relations activities.

Our four children, Kitty, Ed, Chip, and Libby, were born in Mt. Vernon. Chip only lived four days.

In the office at Mt. Vernon, Ohio, PPG plant during the 1950s

The '60s

MY NEXT ASSIGNMENT was in Crystal City, Missouri. At that time, it was the largest glass plant in the company. They produced not only glass but windows for autos. They had some union-management problems in maintenance that we worked through and reached a new agreement. I think I was pretty lucky to hit on some things there and at Mt. Vernon that both sides liked and which solved some nagging labor-management problems.

We were in Crystal City all during the 1960s. It was a nice small town in which to raise children during that tumultuous period of time. When we left in 1970, we left our oldest behind, at the University of Missouri.

The '70s through 2008

I WAS TRANSFERRED to the general office in Pittsburgh for human resources in the glass division. There I got into a number of other things that were very interesting. One was a new company-wide job evaluation and salary structure system. I represented glass on the corporate committee that worked with a consultant. Another big one was when our human resource director became ill, I was named acting director. Then when our director retired, another person in our department was named director of human resources for glass. I wasn't too disappointed. He was more experienced in labor relations than I was. Because we would be participating in multiplant contract negotiations with the union representing seven of our glass plants, I understood.

As it turned out, I was lucky that I didn't get the promotion. At the same time, another opportunity presented itself. I wouldn't have been available for the position if I had been named director. This one was much more appealing to me. The foreign subsidiaries had been reporting to the corporate office staff. Management decided to push that down. Thus, the vice president of the glass division would have all glass operations worldwide, the chemical operations vice president would have all the chemical operations worldwide, and the vice president of the coatings and resins division (paint) the same. My new boss informed me that the corporate vice president of human resources and the department directors of HR were going to visit the corporate headquarters of all the subsidiaries.

Our new director came back from that trip and told me that this would require some attention and that he was going to have the glass subsidiaries report to me for human resources. I'd have to make a trip to all the foreign locations and meet their human resources people.

The HR director also told me after his trip that the corporate general manager of HR in France was female. We'd been trying to promote females and get them developed, but we hadn't been able to get them to that level yet. Thus, I was looking forward to meeting the first female corporate director of HR. But lo, before I could get there, she died of a heart attack.

They brought the HR director from their biggest plant to be her replacement. That was probably a big break for me. He and I really hit it off. He was working on his English, and I was working on my French. It worked out. With Italy, it also went well. Both men spoke some English, and their secretaries spoke English also. It was a big advantage for me to see how HR was handled in various countries.

We were going to build a new glass plant in China in one of the new *industrial zones*. Our VP involved called me in to say that we will be sending people over to train the Chinese. This would include foremen, technicians, etc. Those folks were going to have concerns. Where were their families going to live? What about their children's schooling? And they needed the details about moving to China. He sent me over there to get answers to these questions and to learn other details essential for our people.

Deng Xiaoping, the national secretary of the Communist Party, was the man who ran things then. He had established industrial zones to get foreign investments. Our plant was located in an industrial zone, across the bay from the New Territories, a British colony above Hong Kong. I went to Hong Kong and then to the plant site by hovercraft with an engineer on the project.

A Chinese accountant who spoke English took me around to find the answers to the questions. She was delightful. When we stopped on a low wall to rest, she asked what a good English name would be for her. Her name was Wei Zhang. Usually the English-sounding name other people used was the name of someone they knew or one that sounded like their Chinese name. So I said, "How about Wendy?"

She said, "Is a good name?"

I said, "Well, it's my boss's youngest daughter's name, and recently there was a popular song 'Wendy' (later I discovered it was Windy), and Wendy's has the best hamburgers." She said okay, and within, a week one of our engineers came to my office with her business card, "Wendy Zhang, Accountant." I was very pleased to have given somebody a name! I was fortunate to get to go to China.

So the promotion that I didn't get—the HR director job—somehow I didn't feel too bad about it at all. There was no way I could have had this foreign involvement had I been the HR director. That was a lucky, luckity break!

In the army, I had gotten into the personnel field. And when I got out, I found a job involving that. I had some very good successes. The one disappointment ended up being lucky for me as I received the *foreign* assignment. In my career, *personnel* worked for me!

I retired from PPG after thirty-nine years. At the time, Pittsburgh Presbyterian Theological Seminary needed some help with personnel. So I volunteered. In 2008, I received the John Anderson Award of Merit from the Seminary for my service.

Hand of God

IN VARIOUS CHURCH settings, I've heard references to "the hand of God," especially in talking to teenagers about God's plan for their life. Looking back over these *lucky breaks*, I can't help but feel that the hand of God was involved. Looking back at the whole series in my lifetime—starting with the scholarship to Pitt, choosing ROTC, then getting involved with army personnel, coming back and getting my master's, getting a job in that field, then having breaks at PPG—I know it *had* to be the hand of God. When I look back over how all these things fit together, it had to be God's plan for my life. I am grateful, and I say, "Praise the Lord, and thank You!"

Paul about 100 years old

About the Author

DAUGHTER OF PAUL Schaughency, Kitty lives with her husband, Les, and dogs in the Midwest. She is the mother of three and grandmother of four. She is an avid reader, enjoys discovering stories of her ancestors, and is a member of several lineage societies. Les and Kitty enjoy traveling, going on train rides, attending the local AA baseball games, and visiting both national and state parks. They have been to all the state parks in their state and have been to several state parks in surrounding states. They have a goal of riding a train in all fifty states. They are over halfway to their goal. Their newest interest is camping in their RV.

www.ingramcontent.com/pod-product-compliance
Lightning Source LLC
Chambersburg PA
CBHW040117150726
48005CB00013B/1749